# Classical Music
## for the
# UKULELE

*More than **40** of the world's
most beautiful and enduring
light classic masterpieces.*

ARRANGED BY

## DICK SHERIDAN

To access audio visit:
**www.halleonard.com/mylibrary**

Enter Code
6824-6588-6440-1512

Design & Typography by Roy "Rick" Dains

ISBN 978-1-57424-308-6

 # TRACK LISTING

**T**o enhance your enjoyment of this book, audio tracks for each song are available online. You'll find this especially helpful if you're unfamiliar with a particular piece. Songs are clearly presented to allow you to play along with either the melody or the chords at the suggested tempo, or simply to enjoy listening to the song.

# LIST OF COMPOSERS AND THEIR WORKS

**BACH**
*Minuet*

**BEETHOVEN**
*Allegretto*
*Für Elise*
*Minuet In G*

**BRAHMS**
*Cradle Song*
*Hungarian Dance*
*Waltz In A Flat*

**CHOPIN**
*Fantaisie-Impromptu*
*Prelude In A*

**DVORÁK**
*Largo*
*Humoreske*

**GOUNOD**
*Waltz From "Faust"*

**GRIEG**
*Norwegian Dance*

**HAYDN**
*Andante*

**LEHÁR**
*Merry Widow Waltz*

**LEMARE**
*Andantino*

**LISZT**
*Liebestraum*

**LOUIS XIII**
*Amaryllis*

**MacDOWELL**
*To A Wild Rose*

**MASCAGNI**
*Intermezzo*

**MENDELSSOHN**
*Spring Song*

**MENEGALI – MONTANI**
*Jesu, Salvator Mundi*

**MOZART**
*Rondo Alla Turca*
*Ave Verum Corpus*

**OFFENBACH**
*Barcarolle*

**PONCHIELLI**
*Dance of the Hours*

**ROSAS**
*Over The Waves*

**RUBINSTEIN**
*Melody In F*

**SCHUBERT**
*Serenade*
*Unfinished Symphony*

**SCHUMANN**
*Joyous Farmer*
*Kinderszenen*

**SAINT-SAENS**
*My Heart At Thy Sweet Voice*
*The Swan*

**TCHAIKOVSKY**
*Piano Concerto No.1*

**THOMAS**
*Raymond*

**VERDI**
*March From Aïda*

**WAGNER**
*Song To The Evening Star*

**WALDTEUFEL**
*Skaters' Waltz*

**WEBER**
*Invitation To The Dance*

# TABLE OF CONTENTS

Nancy Hamilton, 1926
Actress, Playwright, Lyricist,
Director & Producer

PORTRAIT OF NANCY HAMILTON

CLASSICAL MUSIC FOR THE UKULELE

 INTRODUCTION

**W**ho would have thought that the small ukulele with its four short strings and 17 frets could encompass the great masterpieces played by a 100-piece symphony orchestra or the flashing fingers of a piano virtuoso flying over a piano's 88 keys? Moreover, who would have thought that the ukulele player could join the ranks of musicians conservatory trained in classical technique on horns, strings, brass, percussion and woodwinds? Admittedly, there are some limitations, but the uke can hold its own, sharing the basic essentials of all classical music – melody, harmony, and rhythm.

The beautiful classical works that follow – the magnificent "lollypops" of the concert hall and salon – all have the quality of endurance, and in some instances have remained popular for hundreds of years. So captivating are these "light" classics that their themes are frequently heard in the movies, on radio and TV, as commercials, in cartoons and even for video games and ringtones. These are the pieces you find yourself humming or whistling in unguarded moments, the ones you instantly recognize the moment you hear them, even if you don't know their names or who composed them.

Many of these classics have taken on a new identity by switching over to contemporary music as popular songs. You may recognize Dvořák's *Largo* as *"Going Home"* or Tchaikovsky's *Piano Concerto No. 1* as *"Tonight We Love."* The melody of Chopin's *Fantasie-Impromptu* was adapted for *"I'm Always Chasing Rainbows"* and Beethoven's *Andante* became *"Moonlight And Roses."* And once heard who can forget Alan Sherman's 1963 humorous parody of Ponchielli's *Waltz Of The Hours* as *"Hello Muddah, Hello Fahduh"* (a letter from Camp Grenada)?

It should be noted that in arranging the classics for the ukulele, it was occasionally necessary to make a few adaptations. Sometimes the extremely high and low notes stretch beyond the reasonable range of the instrument. Octave jumps are employed, lowering the highs and raising the lows. But the notes are always the same and the essential feel of the piece is never compromised.

Also, because of the range of the ukulele or for ease of playing, some compositions needed to be transposed. For example, Chopin's *Prelude in A* was lowered to the key of F. Rubinstein's *Melody In F* was changed to G, and there are other examples.

Fortunately, with tablature you don't have to be a note reader, although a basic understanding of time values is certainly helpful. Yet even without that ability, the the accompanying audio tracks will guide you through the rhythm and allow you to hear and play along with each recording.

Harmonic backgrounds have been carefully analyzed to assure that the ukulele chords capture the intention of the composer. And what a list of composers there is! Virtually all of the best known ones are represented along with their most recognizable works. Several lesser known composers are also included, and although their names may not be familiar their works certainly are.

From opera to operettas, from waltzes and minuets to country dances and graceful ballets, from early Classicism and Baroque to the more modern and sentimental Romanticism of the 19th century, it's all here and yours for the taking. ***Enjoy!***

# ALLEGRETTO
## From Symphony No. 7

Ukulele tuning: gCEA

LUDWIG van BEETHOVEN
(1770 - 1827)

# AMARYLLIS

Ukulele tuning: gCEA

LOUIS XIII
(1601 - 1643)

LOUIS X111 · AMARYLLIS

CLASSICAL MUSIC FOR THE UKULELE

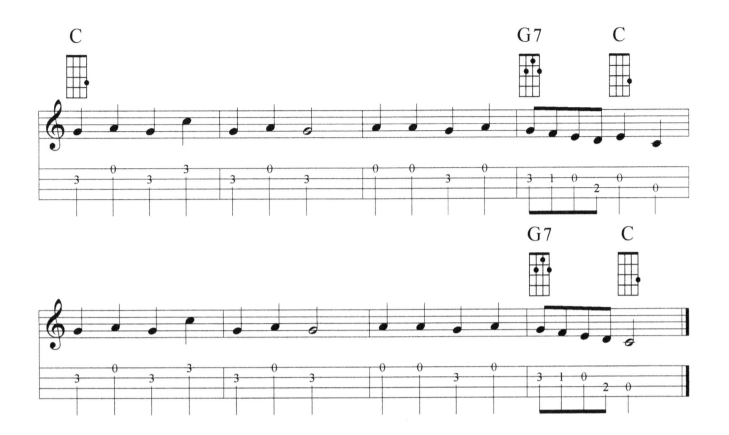

# ANDANTE THEME
## (From "Surprise Symphony" No. 94)

Ukulele tuning: gCEA

JOSEPH HAYDN
(1732 - 1809)

# ANDANTINO
## ("Moonlight and Roses")

Ukulele tuning: gCEA

E. H. LEMARE
(1865 - 1934)

# AVE VERUM CORPUS

Ukulele tuning: gCEA

WOLFGANG AMADEUS MOZART
(1756 - 1791)

# MINUET

## (From Anna Magdalena Notebook)

Ukulele tuning: gCEA

JOHANN SEBASTIAN BACH
(1685 - 1750)

# BARCAROLLE
## (From the opera "The Tales of Hoffmann")

Ukulele tuning: gCEA

JACQUES OFFENBACH
(1819-1880)

OFFENBACH · BARCAROLLE

CLASSICAL MUSIC FOR THE UKULELE

# COUNTRY GARDENS

Ukulele tuning: gCEA

English Folk Melody

# DANCE OF THE HOURS

## (From the Opera "La Gioconda")

Ukulele tuning: gCEA

AMILCARE PONCHIELLI
(1834 - 1886)

**Portrait of Several Musicians and Artists**
*Francois Puget - 1688*

# CRADLE SONG

Ukulele tning: gCEA

JOHANNES BRAHMS
(1813 - 1888)

# INVITATION TO THE DANCE

Ukulele tuning: gCEA

CARL MARIA von WEBER
(1786 - 1826)

# FÜR ELISE

Ukulele tuning: gCEA

LUDWIG van BEETHOVEN
(1770 - 1827)

# HUMORESKE

Ukulele tuning: gCEA

ANTON DVORÁK
(1841 - 1904)

DVORÁK · HUMORESKE

CLASSICAL MUSIC FOR THE UKULELE

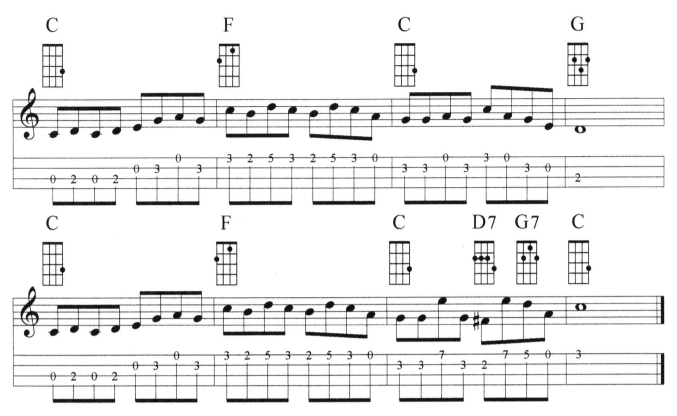

**Bill Tapia**
*Singer, Musician, Ukulele Player*

*Unknown Ukulele Aficionado*

# HUNGARIAN DANCE NO. 5

Ukulele tuning: gCEA

JOHANNES BRAHMS
(1833 - 1897)

BRAHMS · HUNGARIAN DANCE NO. 5

CLASSICAL MUSIC FOR THE UKULELE

# I'M ALWAYS CHASING RAINBOWS
## (Adapted from Frédéric Chopin's "Fantaisie-Impromptu")

Ukulele tuning: gCEA

JOSEPH McCARTHY

HARRY CARROLL

CHOPIN · FANTAISIE-IMPROMPTU

CLASSICAL MUSIC FOR THE UKULELE

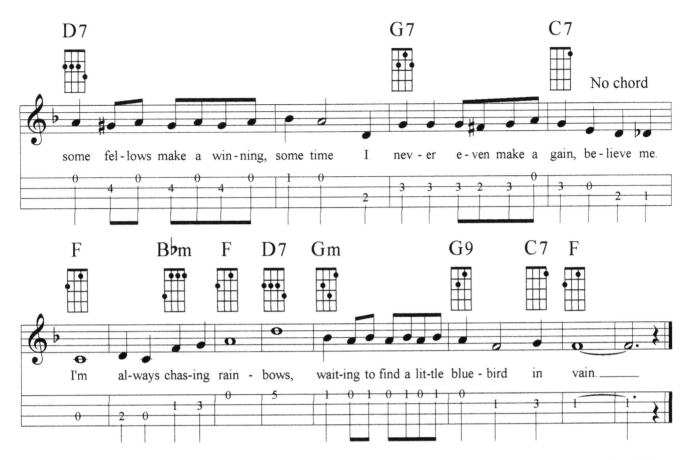

some fel-lows make a win-ning, some time I nev-er e-ven make a gain, be-lieve me.

I'm al-ways chas-ing rain - bows, wait-ing to find a lit-tle blue-bird in vain._____

# INTERMEZZO
## (Fron the opera "Cavalleria rusticana")

Ukulele tuning: gCEA

PIETRO MASCAGNI
(1863 - 1945)

MASCAGNI · INTERMEZZO

CLASSICAL MUSIC FOR THE UKULELE

Jacques Offenbach

Pietro Mascagni

Amilcare Ponchielli

# MELODY IN F
## (Transposed to G)

Ukulele tuning: gCEA

ANTON RUBINSTEIN

(1829 - 1894)

RUBINSTEIN · MELODY IN F

CLASSICAL MUSIC FOR THE UKULELE

# MERRY WIDOW WALTZ

Ukulele tuning: gCEA

FRANZ LEHÁR
(1870-1948)

# JESU, SALVATOR MUNDI

Ukulele tuning: gCEA

MENEGALI - MONTANI

♩=100

Je - su,   Sal - va - tor mun - di,   tu - is   fa - mu - lis

sub - ve - ni,   quos pre - ti - o - so   san - gui - ne,   quos pre - ti - o - so

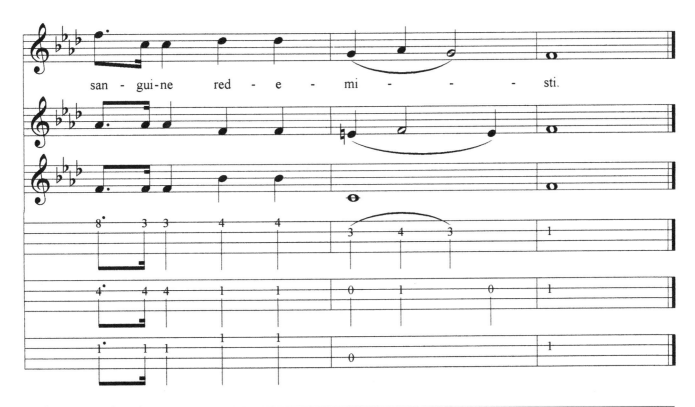

san - gui-ne red - e - mi - sti.

**Presentation of Christ at the Temple**
*Philippe de Champaigne - 1648*

MONTANI · JESU, SALVATOR MUNDI

# THE JOYOUS FARMER

Ukulele tuning: gCEA

ROBERT SCHUMANN
(1810 - 1856)

SCHUMANN · THE JOYOUS FARMER

CLASSICAL MUSIC FOR THE UKULELE

# KINDERSZENEN

## OPUS 14

## Von fremden Ländern und Menschen

Ukulele tuning: gCEA

ROBERT SCHUMANN
(1810 - 1856)

Pyotor Tchaikovsky

Franz Liszt

# LARGO
## "Going Home"
### From the New World Symphony

Ukulele tuning: gCEA

ANTONIN DVORÁK
(1841 - 1904)

DVORÁK · LARGO

# LIEBESTRAUM

Ukulele tuning: gCEA

FRANZ LISZT
(1811 - 1886)

# MARCH FROM AÏDA

Ukulele tuning: gCEA

GIUSEPPE VERDI
(1813 - 1901)

# MY HEART AT THY SWEET VOICE

Ukulele tuning: gCEA

C. SAINT-SAENS

Source: Songtime

# NORWEGIAN DANCE

Ukulele tuning: gCEA

EDVARD GRIEG
(1843 - 1907)

# MINUET IN G

Ukulele tuning: gCEA

LUDWIG van BEETHOVEN
(1770 - 1827)

# PIANO CONCERTO No.1

## (Theme)

Ukulele tuning: gCEA

PYOTR ILYITCH TCHAIKOVSKY
(1840 - 1893)

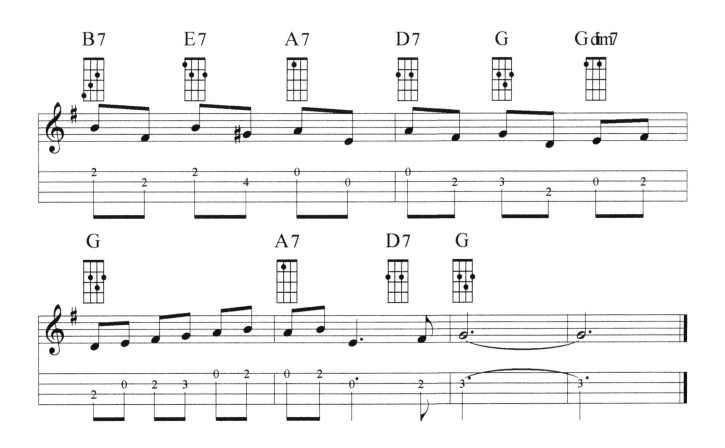

# SONG TO THE EVENING STAR

Ukulele tuning: gCEA

RICHARD WAGNER

(1813 - 1883)

# UNFINISHED SYMPHONY

## (Theme)

Ukulele tuning: gCEA

FRANZ SCHUBERT

(1797 - 1828)

# RONDO
## Alla Turca

Ukulele tuning: gCEA

WOLFGANG AMADEUS MOZART
(1756 - 1791)

MOZART · RONDO ALLA TURCA

CLASSICAL MUSIC FOR THE UKULELE

# SERENADE

Ukulele tuning: gCEA

FRANZ SCHUBERT
(1797 - 1828)

# SKATERS' WALTZ
## (Les Patineurs)

Ukulele tuning: gCEA

ÉMIL WALDTEUFEL
(1837 - 1915)

# SPRING SONG

Ukulele tuning: gCEA

FELIX MENDELSSOHN
(1809 - 1846)

MENDELSSOHN · SPRING SONG

CLASSICAL MUSIC FOR THE UKULELE

Joseph Haydn

Felix Mendelssohn

# THE SWAN

Ukulele tuning: gCEA

CAMILLE SAINT-SAENS
(1835 - 1921)

SAINT-SAENS · THE SWAN

CLASSICAL MUSIC FOR THE UKULELE

# RAYMOND

## (From the overture to the French opera)

Ukulele tuning: gCEA

AMBROISE THOMAS
(1811 - 1896)

# TO A WILD ROSE

Op. 51 No. 1
From Woodland Sketches

Ukulele tuning: gCEA

EDWARD MacDOWELL
(1860 - 1908)

MACDOWELL · TO A WILD ROSE

CLASSICAL MUSIC FOR THE UKULELE

# OVER THE WAVES

## (Sobre Las Olas)

Ukulele tuning: gCEA

JUVENTINO ROSAS
*(1868 - 1894)*

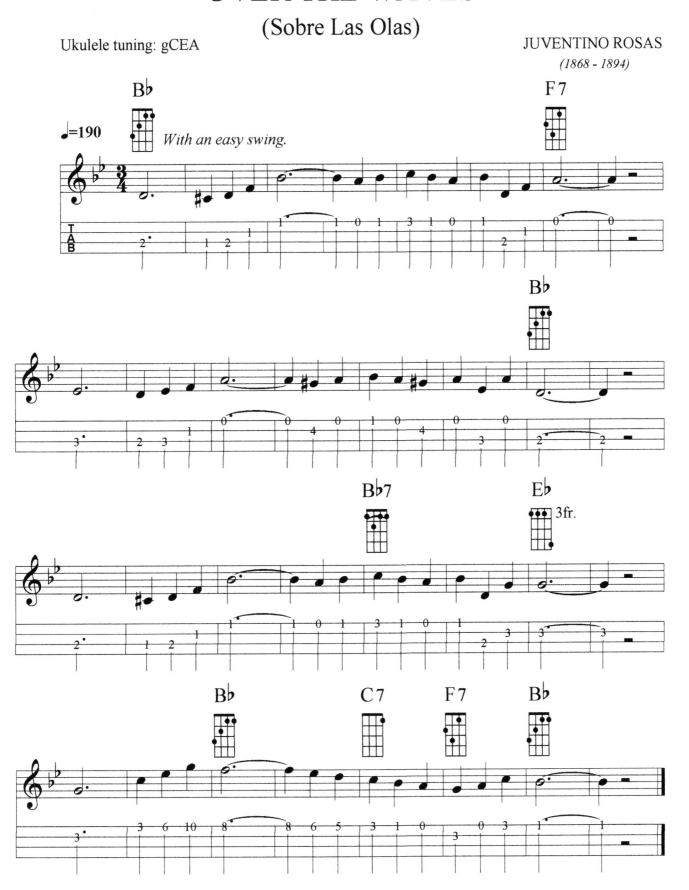

# WALTZ
## (Theme from the Opera "Faust")

Ukulele tuning: gCEA

CHARLES GOUNOD
(1818 - 1893)

# WALTZ IN A FLAT
## (Transposed to D)

Ukulele tuning: gCEA

JOHANNES BRAHMS
(1833 - 1897)

# PRELUDE IN A
## Op. 28, No. 7
## (Transposed to F)

Ukulele tuning: gCEA

FRÉDÉRIC CHOPIN
(1810 - 1849)

Dick Sheridan grew up in a musical household where both his parents played the piano. Although not professional musicians, they were accomplished amateurs and their playing was a constant source of family enjoyment and entertainment. His father, who could play by ear, favored popular songs. His mother, strictly a note reader, preferred the classics and would typically play several hours a day.

The family never had a real phonograph, and apart from the piano, exposure to the classics came mainly from New York City's classical radio station WQXR. There was, however, a vintage hand-me-down Victrola that contained a small selection of 78 rpm Victor Red Seal classical records with songs by early opera stars, popular singers of the World War I era, and scratchy instrumental recordings. The wind-up Victrola also boasted two albums, Grieg's Peer Gynt Suite and one of keyboard selections by José Iturbi. Dick points out that radio listening is still a source of enjoyment for him and that he is fortunate to have a local public broadcasting station in Syracuse, NY– WCNY's "Classic FM" -- that airs the classics 24 hours a day.

Dick shared his parents' love of music, both popular and classical, but not their interest in playing the piano. Instead he gravitated to the fretted string instruments, the first being a small soprano ukulele given to him when he was in grade school. He went on to play the folk guitar, the baritone uke, 5-string banjo, and the tenor banjo which he plays with a Dixieland jazz band that he has led for over 40 years. His fascination with the ukulele has never waned. He currently plays a concert and a baritone uke, often joining with friends at gatherings and sessions, as well as playing for his own enjoyment. Dick has written several collections of ukulele arrangements for Centerstream Publishing some of which are listed elsewhere in this book.

Other than listening to the classics on radio and TV, on recordings, or in the concert hall, Dick had no other way to enjoy these great works -- until he found they were adaptable to the uke and that he could now play them himself. This opened up not only a new direction for him but also a new dimension for the ukulele as well.

Creating this book has proved a special pleasure for Dick, one that he is eager to share with you. You'll find that you too can discover the excitement and satisfaction that come from being able to make these immortal classics your own. Truly, a fascinating world of fun and enjoyment exists right at your finger tips.

# More Great Ukulele Books from Centerstream...

# More Great Books from Dick Sheridan...

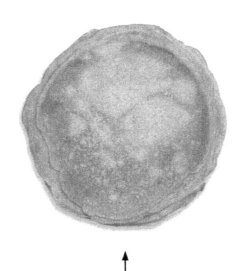

The Competition

Those using
Centerstream
Books & DVDs